So, you want to photograph a wedding?

The essential guide for anyone who wants to photograph a wedding

GRANT HAYWOOD

I0470389

Contents

Introduction

If you are a wedding photographer wondering how to streamline your work, or someone thinking of becoming a wedding photographer, or even someone who has a camera and has been asked to photograph a friend's wedding, this is the book for you. At the end of it, you will all have the same information, the only thing separating you now is talent.

About the Author

Grant and Samantha Haywood have been photographing weddings for 20 years. Grant grew up with a strong interest in photography and a will to learn. Encouraged by his father, who is also a keen photographer, he learned his trade. His first camera, a Brownie box camera leading to a Zenith E that travelled the world with him. His late brother who was also a talented photographer would be his greatest critic and keep him learning. He learned various techniques from both his brother and father and adapted them to be his own.

Always having a camera to hand, often talking about wanting to become a wedding photographer, finally meeting the one person who would make that happen. In 1995 Grant met Samantha who became his wife. She had the drive and determination to empower him to become the photographer he wanted to be. With her drive and the influence from his brother and father his work improved and continued to do so.

Grant finally met the late Graham Wiseman, who was a professional photographer and had been since the 1960's. Graham being the man he was decided to train Grant. He took him to every wedding, explained what was going on and allowed him to take photographs. Gradually more of Grant's photographs were used in Graham's final work until eventually Graham retired and Grant took over the studio.

The studio ran for a few more years until wedding photography became the main business and the studio was closed.

Samantha became Grant's assistant (although she may tell it the other way around), and art director. Her keen eye for detail ensured that every wedding was photographed with almost military precision, nothing was missed, every image scrutinised for fault and honed to perfection. She developed techniques to photograph large groups of people in just a few minutes instead of the extraordinary amount of time that it used to take.

Grant has now placed all of this experience and learning into this book. The book assumes that you have already learned to use a camera and have developed the necessary skills to operate all of the equipment. It explains in detail the substance of a wedding, what to look for and when to look for it. With this guide, anyone capable of using a camera will be able to photograph a wedding and produce exceptional results.

It will take you from the first phone call from the Bride and Groom to the final production of a set of images that any wedding photographer would be proud of. He has kept techno speak to a minimum and told you exactly how it is done.

Introduction to Wedding Photography

Wedding photography is not easy. For some of you who have no previous experience, the prospect is perhaps daunting but also a little exciting. Those of you who have some experience already know how important and challenging this branch of photography is.

Most of you have probably been asked to take photographs at a friend or relatives wedding at some time or another. Usually this request is for additional candid shots to complement those taken by the official photographer. It is quite easy to be relaxed on these occasions because the official photographer is organising the set pieces and if your photographs are not successful the only thing to suffer is your reputation as an amateur photographer.

However, when you are the official photographer the situation is totally different since you have a contract with the bride and groom to provide the official photographs and you only get one chance to get it right.

You must ensure that you are professional enough to cope with the many problems which can arise, particularly with people who are understandably nervous on the day which may have been planned for months, or even years. It is your job to be calm and in control of what you have to do. You will seldom have more than 45 minutes to capture the main part of the day photographically. There is no time check in the back of your camera after each shot if you want to keep to schedule and maintain a rapport with your subjects.

If anything goes wrong with your equipment or schedule, the wedding cannot be run another day and the magic of the couples day will be lost forever. In addition, news of your failure will spread like wildfire. Since more people than ever are resorting to litigation for poor service, your wedding photography must be absolutely professional and this can only be achieved by your **preparation, technique, and knowledge of your equipment.**

The aim of this book is to enable you to achieve a professional standard of photography with some basic skills which you can then develop as you gain more experience. The service that you offer as a professional MUST be different from the pictures taken by every other amateur with a camera or smartphone at the wedding, that is if you are to sell the results. Please be open minded as the book progresses since you will learn more and consolidate the knowledge which you may already possess.

Equipment

Your camera equipment may well be new, and will most likely have been expensive, but sooner or later it WILL break down. If you face this fact now, disasters can be avoided. It is no use saying "but the camera was alright last week" when you're standing in front of the church with 200 people lined up for a photograph and you can't take any photo's due to equipment failure. It is simply too late.

Carry out the following checks before every wedding and make sure that your equipment is operating correctly. These tests should cover everything apart from the camera jamming or being dropped on the day. If this happens, simply change over to a spare unit which has also been tested.

2 Cameras   **Flash Sync –**   Check that this is set to 'AUTO FP' or similar, and not manual. The majority of failures on the day are due to the flash sync not being correctly set.

Shutter -   Before the wedding, fire the camera at all shutter speeds from 1 second up to 1/500 sec. You will soon spot a shutter that is beginning to stick as this fault will usually appear on the slower speeds first which are not normally used and then spreads to the faster speeds.

Aperture leaves -   Check that all the aperture leaves are fully opening and closing.

Focus -   Focus the camera on infinity and look through the viewfinder at an object over 200 feet away. If the object appears sharp, then in all probability the camera is undamaged.

Cleanliness-   Clean the lenses and viewfinder before use. Always clean the inside of the camera before use.

2 Flash guns   **Charging -**   Make sure that the flash guns are charged the day before the wedding.

Sync leads -   If using sync leads for off camera flash, make sure that you have at least two spare leads for each gun.

Cleanliness -   Clean battery contacts.

Spare equipment   The importance of having spare equipment cannot be over emphasised. A photographer who leaves his spare camera at home, only to find his main camera faulty during a wedding needs shooting. Any spare cameras or flashes that you have should be taken with you.

A tripod can come in useful should you have flash problems you can use the tripod for slower shutter speeds available light shots which is safer than hand held.

Real World equipment

Please remember that today's wedding photography is very mobile and animated. Gone are the days when the photographer is expected to stand behind a tripod while guests are lined up in front of them. Now you need to be very mobile, very versatile, and very quick. Guests do not like to be kept waiting whilst the photographs are taken.

You will need as a minimum;

- ❖ Two DSLR digital cameras

Camera one, which should be your main camera will need an on camera flash and ideally a f2.8 28 – 70mm lens, and a double card reader for instantaneous back up.

Camera two, this is your 'long shot' camera, will also need an on camera flash and ideally a f2.8 70-300mm lens. A double card reader would be nice, but not as essential.

- ❖ Eight 4gb memory cards, all formatted

We use 4gb cards rather than larger ones because if a card fails, you will lose less of the day. Imagine a scenario where you have photographed an entire wedding on one 32gb card, and the card fails, is damaged or is lost or stolen.

- ❖ Two batteries for each camera
- ❖ Two sets of batteries for each flash unit

Depending on the location and photography requirements you may also want to carry a wide-angle lens for table shots, and very large groups shots, a reflector for portraits, a 50mm lens for portraits, and extra flash units for off camera flash.

All of the above can be carried on your person all day long which makes you very mobile. However some or all of the equipment listed above can fail. So you will need at least one backup for everything listed. This can be left in the car or carried by an assistant and collected if needed. All backup equipment should be charged and tested just the same as the main equipment.

Check the time and date on every camera and ensure that they are all synchronised, this will save you hours of work in post production.

An Assistant

I have decided to include the assistant in this section because out of all the equipment that you have at your disposal, he or she will become the most valuable. They need to know as much if not more about the plans than you do, they need to be very good at organising large groups of people without the need to shout at them, they may need to carry some of your kit, they need to be able to learn names and put faces to them, they need to be able to spot potential photo opportunities when you may be looking the other way. On the day, your job is to follow the bride, your assistants job is to watch everyone else, whilst at the same time looking out for you.

They may also need to be able to take a good photograph because it would be foolhardy to have an assistant on site and not give them a camera.

Photographic Technique

The object of this section is to recommend a technique which is especially safe for wedding photography. Weddings need a special approach – you can't go back tomorrow to re-take an image and you won't have time to re-take any of the images on the day. For this reason, the techniques used may differ from those used for other forms of photography.

General Rules

Never use a shutter speed of less than 1/125 of a second unless it is for available light church interior shots or for window light portrait of the bride – both of these can be taken under controlled conditions. Some photographers like to work on a manual setting with a light meter, others like to use the camera's auto setting. Given that modern digital SLR cameras are now very sophisticated either should be fine. Be aware that light conditions can change rapidly so if shooting manually you will need to be taking light readings regularly. If shooting on auto, remember that the camera can't see what you can. It only sees shades of grey so it may be necessary to change shutter speeds and/or aperture, and/or iso settings – Do not assume that the camera's software is able to cater for every eventuality.

Exposures

You will usually encounter four different exposures outside the church. Learn this list by heart, and if a meter goes wrong on the day, with care, you will avoid disasters.

1/125 at F16 or F11	-	Always sunny conditions with usually harsh shadows – fill in flash required.
1/125 at F8	-	Sunny, but hazy bright conditions, no harsh shadows. Ideal for available light exposures.
1/125 at F5.6	-	Again, hazy bright available light.
1/125 at F4	-	Decision time; If the subject looks bright and the reading is slightly above F4 then shoot available light. If the subject looks dull and the reading is below F4 then shoot direct flash as if indoors. BUT make sure the subjects are against a background, not in the middle of a field and avoid any sky in the picture.

FILL IN FLASH

Auto flash guns – Set the aperture indicator on the flash gun to about two stops more than the actual aperture used on the camera, i.e. if the exposure on the camera is set to 1/125 at F11, set the flash gun to F5.6. This will result in the flashgun under exposing and thus giving a pleasant fill-in effect.

Manual flashguns – Use of the full and half power switch on your gun will enable you to adjust the relative flash and camera settings to have the effect of the flash under exposing by 1-1/2 to 2 stops. Each flash will vary in power and will require a different technique.

Golden Rule – When using flash outdoors never equal out the flash with the available light exposure, or use a shutter speed of less than 1/125 sec. Both can easily result in 'double image' effect which looks out of focus to the eye. Wedding photographs are very prone to this defect, and as fill in flash is such an important part of your technique do ensure that you are competent.

Framing – Always focus on the eyes, and then compose the picture in the viewfinder, and then fire the shutter. Many pictures can be spoilt if the image is too low in the frame. A good motto to remember is;

FOCUS – FRAME – FIRE

Indoor Flash

The golden rule is to KEEP IT SIMPLE. Use direct flash all the time except for mirror shots, when you could double up with bounce flash. Bounce flash will look more natural, but even the most experienced photographer can slip up. If you are careful to avoid reflections, direct flash is adequate. Whether you decide to use manual flash or automatic flash is up to you. Manual flash is more accurate, but in general, failure rate is probably lower with auto flash.

The main problem with auto flash is over reliance on it, and the main problem with manual is forgetting to alter aperture.

Direction of flash is also important – mid directed flash can produce almost unprintable results. The angle of the beam on some modern flash guns is very narrow, and great care should be taken if the gun is used off the camera (hand held). Our golden rule for this is **check the direction of the flash before taking each photograph.** If you use flash on camera, be careful of red eye. This happens when the flash is too close in angle to the taking lens of the camera.

If you are using a camera with blind operation you will not be able to see the if the flash actually fires – in this case take great care to note the re-cycling noise from the flash gun. This can be very quiet with some modern flash guns so be careful.

Watch out for background shadows – if possible, stand your subject a little away from backgrounds.

The first meeting

When taking the first phone call have a pre-designed form by the phone, or in your diary. You need to get as much information as possible before you meet the couple. As a minimum you need the following;

- ❖ Name of Bride and Groom
- ❖ Address and contact details
- ❖ Date and time of the wedding
- ❖ Location of the wedding
- ❖ Location of the reception, if different from the wedding
- ❖ Number of guests
- ❖ Required style of photography

Your wedding photography begins on the day you meet the bride and groom. Turn up on time, dressed smartly either in uniform if you have one, or in a suit. Personally, I prefer to wear branded uniform, this makes us instantly recognisable to guests, advertises the company, and it won't ruin a good suit when you're lying on wet grass trying to get just the right angle.

This meeting can be a year before the actual wedding day. Know your product. When you do meet them they will ask you many questions, you need to know the answers. If you don't, tell them that you don't know but will find out. Many couples will assume that you know the venue that they have chosen and ask questions about it. So if the venue is one you have not been to, go there and see it for yourself before you meet the couple. You are far more likely to get the job if you have been to the venue. If it is one that you have used before, take samples of your images along to show them.

A good wedding photographer should help make the day go more smoothly. Aside from a dedicated wedding planner, the photographer is the only vendor who is going to be spending the entire day with the Bride and Groom. A good wedding photographer should make things easier for them. They should solve problems. The wedding photographer should be flexible. They should be able to adapt and thrive in difficult situations

Spend as much time as you can with the couple at this initial meeting, get to know them, and allow them to know you. They are not only deciding whether to employ you as a photographer, they are also deciding whether to invite you to their wedding. Ask them what they have planned for the day. You need to know every detail about their wedding, on the day of the wedding you will have a lot to do and you **absolutely do not want any surprises**. Apart from the information above, you should also ask for the following;

- ❖ Name and contact details of the person who is organising the day - *(this is usually someone who works for the venue but may be a professional wedding planner)*
- ❖ Time of the wedding breakfast and how many courses
- ❖ Time of the speeches *(this will tell you how much time you have after the ceremony to get the majority of your images)*
- ❖ Number of Bridesmaids and Groomsmen
- ❖ How many suits *(this can be different from above, basically you need to know how many men will be dressed in the same suit and wearing the same flower because at some point they will want to be photographed together)*
- ❖ Number of page boys / flower girls
- ❖ Time of the cutting of the cake
- ❖ Time of the first dance
- ❖ Is the first dance straight forward, or is the Bride planning to bungie jump onto the dance floor – I have seen this done so make sure you ask the question.

- ❖ Will there be other entertainment for the guests? (*children's entertainers, bouncy castles, celebrities, photo booths, drones, fireworks etc*) they will have paid for these services and will want to see photographs of them
- ❖ If possible, ask to speak to the Bride and Groom separately, they may have arranged something as a surprise for each other in which case you need to know
- ❖ Will there be a videographer, if so you will need to work closely with them to ensure that he/she is not in all of your photographs, and that you are not in all of their videos. If possible get the videographers details and speak to them before the day.
- ❖ How will the Bride and Groom be arriving at the venue – again, you will not want to miss this?
- ❖ Are both sets of parents alive and will they be at the wedding? *(You don't want to be calling for father of the bride only to find out that he died last year – this will really ruin your brides makeup and your photographs).*
- ❖ If there is a family separation, will both parents agree to appear in the same image and be happy at the prospect? Check to see if there are any step-parents and how the relationships are between people.

Some of this information may not be available at this stage, but by asking the questions you will be proving that you are interested, capable, and experienced. Design an information form with your logo and details on it. Leave a copy with the couple and make absolutely sure that you have it returned and completed at least one month before the wedding.

Many couples will invite you to eat with them at the reception. My advice would be to decline. If you are eating at the reception it is uncomfortable for the guests whose table you are at. You will not be able to relax as you will feel that you are still working and odds are the couple only asked because they feel obliged to. Since no one, and I mean absolutely no-one wants to be photographed whilst they are eating, this time is far better used for you and your assistant to take a break.

Nearly all couples have a list in their head of photographs they would like to have taken. This can be set groups, images that their friends had done, images from your website, general images they have seen on Google. The latter will be the most difficult to replicate as most have been done under controlled conditions with controlled lighting using models. Your Bride and Groom will not accept that they won't look like the models you are trying to replicate. You need this list. Have them write it down and work to it, it is your bible for the day. Talk to the couple about any images that are not possible due to location, lack of facilities, time of year, available light etc. For instance; If the couple have found an image taken over a lake with their reflection on the water and want one the same, this won't work without a lake.

Once complete, this list needs to be copied and given to all of the groomsmen and bridesmaids. They are going to be your extra unpaid staff. It is in their job description for the day that they are there to assist the Bride and Groom, they also have the added advantage of knowing all or most of the names on the list, therefore, who better to assist when looking for the brides second cousin because she is on the list of required images?

Once the couple have agreed to employ you, you need to establish payment. Most people now will use bank transfer. You need to take a deposit to secure the day, usually £100 will be sufficient at this stage. As soon as the money is in your bank, issue a receipt and make a note in your diary against the couples details. Ideally you will need the balance payment one month before the date of the wedding. This gets the money out of the way, into your bank, and is one less thing for you or the couple to worry about on the day.

One month before the wedding

At this point your Bride and Groom will be in a state of mild panic, bordering on hysteria. They have only four weeks to make sure that all of their plans have been planned correctly and that they haven't missed anything out.

Call them or visit them. You will be calm and you will have the all-important list. Go through the list with them item by item and if anything has been missed, you will highlight it. This is also an ideal opportunity for you to check that nothing has changed, like the venue or the name of the Groom, and give a gentle reminder that the balance is now due to be paid to your account.

Reassure your Bride, I say Bride now because at this point in time your Groom has gone into meltdown and the best we can hope for from him now is that he turns up sober, dressed appropriately, on time, and helps keep the sun off the Brides face during the photography.

Go through the whole day with her and assure her that you have all of the timings for the day, that you have spoken to the venue organiser and that it absolutely will run like clockwork.

You are not going to be just her wedding photographer, you are going to be her wedding co-ordinator, and you are going to ensure that all of her plans for the day come to fruition. It will be you or your assistant that helps her with her hair, her flowers, her dress, her shoes and it will be you who keeps track on where she left her drink or her bag. If it gets cold it will be you who knows where her jacket is. As her photographer it will be your job to follow the bride always where possible keeping her in view, the groom whilst sober will be doing the same so, as long as you can see her, he won't be too far away. And on the day every single guest will talk to at least one of them which means you will or should have a photograph of every single guest.

During this phone call or visit, you need to convey all of this and more with a look, or a very short, reassuring sentence.

Going through the day with the Bride and telling her what will be happening at each stage will reassure her that it will all be alright on the day. You will become her rock for the day, the one person at her wedding that knows every single detail of the wedding as well as she does.

Now let's look at those details a little closer.

The day before the wedding

Your first job is to get out every piece of equipment that you intend to take with you remove every battery, every memory card, and all of the lenses.

Charge all of the batteries and ensure that you do not mix up the charged with the discharged. This is not only common sense, it will also give you piece of mind on the day.

Whilst the batteries are charging, clean each lens and replace the caps, check each lens for operation. Clean each camera inside and out. There are many products on the market to help with this, but I usually find that a clean cloth and a clean soft paint brush are good enough. Personally, I don't like the idea of spraying chemicals onto, or into the camera body, but this is matter of personal preference. Just be sure that the unit is clean and that you are satisfied with the fact that it is clean.

Once done, reassemble the camera's, batteries, lenses and flash units. Use the cameras to format every single memory card and check the operation of each unit as described in section one.

Now your equipment is ready for the wedding, pack it away and leave it alone in a safe place. Preferably away from children, pets, heat sources, and extreme cold.

Make a few copies of the brides list.

Your next job is to make sure that all of your uniform / clothes are ready for the big day. Just as the Bride and Groom are preparing for tomorrow, so must you.

- ❖ Check your car, does it have fuel?
- ❖ Do you know your route?
- ❖ Are all and any postcodes programmed into sat nav?
- ❖ Have you checked the weather?
- ❖ If you have an assistant is he/she as ready as you are?

No matter how long you do this job for, or how many weddings you may have covered, the responsibility that you carry never diminishes. You will only ever be as good as your last wedding and tomorrow you may have 200 people relying on you to be prepared, in control, calm, professional and capable.

Now sit down and read through the brides list for tomorrow.

You do not want any surprises and neither does she.

Sleep well.

The Wedding Day

We are going to look at the wedding day itself by breaking it down into sections. The day for you will be long, tiring, stressful and at times frustrating. In contrast, the day for your Bride and Groom will go very quickly, the only memories they will have of the day will be the ones that you have recorded – so no pressure then.

Brides preparation

It may be that your Bride has asked for Bridal preparation shots. These may be done at home or in a hotel room. In either case remember that you will have no control over the environment. The room will be in chaos, there will be clothes strewn everywhere, there will be hairdressers, makeup artists, bridesmaids, flower girls, flowers, shoes, champagne, and of course the Brides mother. You are going to be in the way, and despite the fact that the Bride has asked you to take these photos, she won't want them done until her makeup is perfect, there will always be at least one Bridesmaid who refuses to have her photograph taken, there will be tears and there will be tantrums.

You still need to produce some stunning images.

This is where your assistant is invaluable, because he/she can be dealing with all of the above, while you are at the venue photographing arriving guests, Groom and groomsmen. You will always get much better images of the Brides preparation if they are taken by a female, for the simple reason that she won't need to leave the room every time someone decides to undress. Not that she would photograph this, but by staying in the room she can control it, whereas a male photographer quite rightly should leave the room but will lose control of the room each time he does therefore losing valuable time.

Examples of some brides preparation shots

- Wedding dress laying over a chair
- Zipping, tying or buttoning the wedding dress
- Mother of the bride fastening the bride's necklace
- The bride's garter
- The bride's veil
- The bride's bouquet
- A close up of the brides shoes peeking out from under the dress
- Bride looking into a mirror
- Bride looking out of window
- Bride and bridesmaids putting on makeup
- Bride pinning corsage/boutonniere on mother/father
- Bride hugging parents
- Bride touching up makeup
- Bride and parents leaving for ceremony
- Bride getting into car
- Female wedding party – sitting on the bed, standing, on the way to the aisle
- Female wedding party with champagne / drinks
- Personal items displayed – Something blue, something borrowed, bouquet, special

jewellery, shoes.

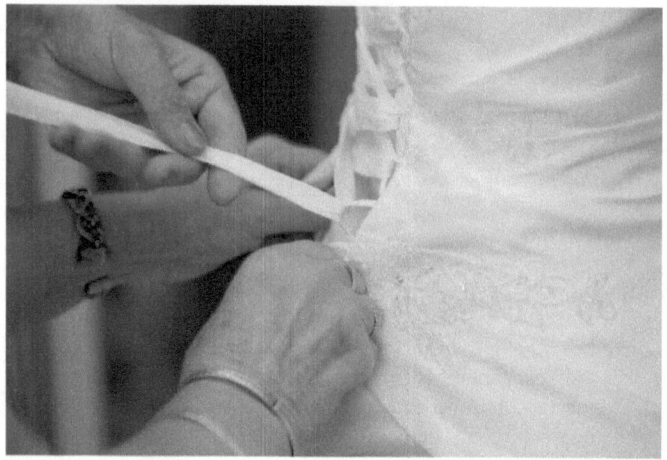

Meanwhile, back at the ranch….

So, whilst your assistant is in charge of the Bridal preparation shots, you can be at the venue. We will assume for a while that the wedding is an all-day event in one location, such as a hotel or specific wedding venue, which would imply that your assistant is in the Bridal suite not too far away.

As soon as you arrive, introduce yourself to the organiser and ask them to show you around. You need to know where the actual wedding will take place, where the reception or wedding breakfast will take place, and at what time will the rooms be ready. Also, whilst you have the opportunity, go through the timings on the list and make sure that you are both singing from the same sheet. As soon as the rooms are ready, you need to get in there and photograph the detail. We will go into more detail of the actual images later in this book.

Your next job is to find the Groom, remind him who you are, and ask him about his Groomsmen. As soon as you can you need to get them all together and get some photographs. It will be a lot easier to get these images now rather than after the ceremony when 200 people are trying to get their attention. At this point you will also need to check that they are all dressed appropriately.

- Are they wearing jackets?
- Do they have hats to wear?
- Do they all have flowers in their lapel?
- Is there an odd one out i.e. one without a coloured cravat, tie, handkerchief?

The Bride will not have planned for an odd one out, so this one needs to be suitably dressed before the photographs are taken.

Once these images are complete and safe, the Groomsmen can be released, probably to the bar, leaving you free to go to the venue entrance and photograph the guests as they arrive.

Photographing people as they arrive has several advantages;

- It introduces you as the official photographer.
- It gets them used to the idea that you will be taking their photograph all day long.
- It gives you an opportunity so find out which guests will be open to photography and which ones will hide in the bar.
- It allows you to identify any large personalities; these people will be useful later when you want to add some fun shots to the collection.
- It helps to ensure that you don't miss anyone out.

So by now we are about half an hour away from the ceremony, and we already have images of the Groomsmen and hopefully most of the guests.

Now, go to the reception room, photograph the detail while the room is empty, then go straight to the ceremony room and do the same.

You will need to speak to the Registrar before the ceremony too, find them and ask what if any rules they may have on photography. In my experience they are all different, some will allow you to photograph anything at any time, others will be very strict.

We should be about 10 minutes away from the ceremony now. Your assistant will be with the Bride and will follow her to the ceremony room taking photographs along the way.

You need to be in the ceremony room.

The guests will be gently filing into the room; The Registrar will be setting up their desk and paperwork. Hopefully your Groom is now standing at, or near, the front of the room along with his best man, your chance to take more natural images of him and the interaction with the guests. Use your long lens too; pick out portraits of the guests.

You probably have two minutes left now, check your messages, if there is anything you need to know, hopefully your assistant will have had the presence of mind to let you know.

TURN YOUR PHONE / VOLUME OFF

You are going to be standing in front of 200 guests. Only you and the Registrar will be facing the crowd, you do not want your phone to ring!

Show time – The Ceremony

In a moment the Registrar will announce the Brides arrival, and ask the guests to stand.

You need to be able to get images of the Brides arrival, her walk down the aisle, her reaction when she sees the Groom and his reaction to seeing her. And you will need to do this with 200 guests all standing in your way and trying to get the same photographs.
You have one advantage – the Registrar.

The Registrar will have a table of some description and it will be positioned front and centre at the end of the aisle. At this moment in time the Registrar will not mind you standing behind the desk in the middle and taking your photographs. You should have a perfect view. Have your camera set for continuous high speed and continuous auto tracking (focus) and get as many shots as you have time for. You are hoping for a look from the Bride or Groom that says everything about the occasion, the tantrums, tears and planning that has brought them to this moment in time.

As soon as she arrives at the 'alter' take one more shot, take your time, you want Bride, Groom, Best man, and father of the bride in a line if possible, if not just go for Bride and Groom, you cannot direct this shot, you just need to hope that they all look in your direction and stand close enough together…..**now get out of the way!**

Hopefully your assistant will have been getting the same shots from the back of the room. Please try and keep out of each other's photographs.

For the next 30 minutes you will have no control over proceedings. Every person in that room will be hanging on every word that the Registrar says, he / she is the boss. It is their room, please never forget this. Stick to the rules, if the Registrar says no photo's, simply put down the camera. However, odds are that the Registrar will allow a few images and they will be standard.

- Speakers
- The rings
- The kiss

If you're fortunate, your Registrar will allow a few more images but it's their show, so just go with their rules. I have seen photographers ignore these rules, it's not pretty. At best you will be asked in front of 200 people to leave the room, at worst you will have the same registrar at your next wedding…..and yes, they will remember you.

So, the ceremony is nearly over, you've got this far without being thrown out; the Registrar is close to handing this room of people back to you. All that is left is to sign the register. I cannot stress this next sentence enough:

IT IS AGAINST THE LAW TO PHOTOGRAPH THE REGISTER AND THE SIGNING OF IT:

Attempting this will land you in a whole world of pain so just move to the back of the room and let them get on with it.

Assuming that you have read the last two sentences, and are still in the room, the next thing to happen will be that the Registrar will hand the room to you. They will signal with a look or nod and expect you to come to the front of the room. Usually they will provide a blank or mock up register for you to use as a prop and the room is yours, for about five minutes.

You have about five minutes to get any shots you want of the signing of the register, again, specific shots will be listed later on in this book.

It is now your turn to hand control back to the Registrar. You see, he or she now needs to dismiss the Bride and Groom, give them a certificate, and dismiss the guests. So now is your chance to use them to your own advantage.

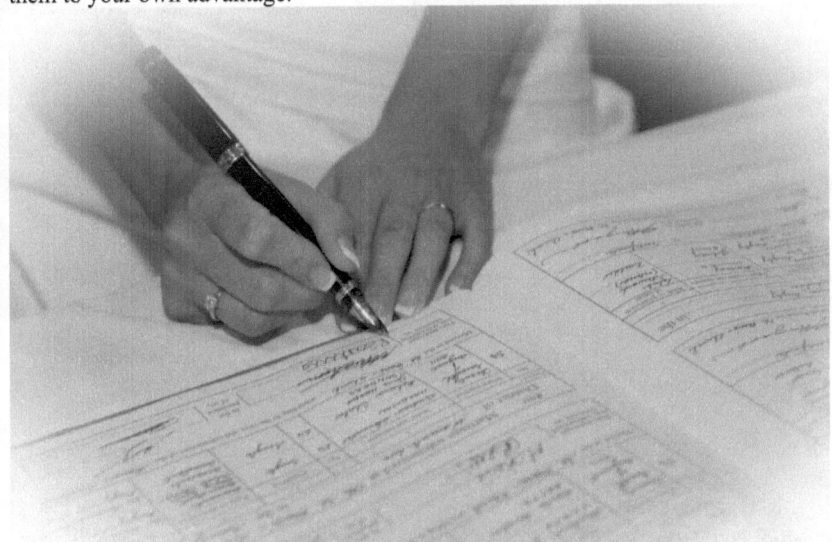

In about five minutes you will need all of the guests and the Bride and Groom to move to an area outside where you can take all of the group photographs on the Brides list. You will most likely only have about 30 to 45 minutes to do this, and everyone in that room is thinking about getting to the bar, once there you will have lost them.

But there is one person in that room that still has control ....the Registrar and he or she is about to address the room. So, go to him or her, thank them, and ask them if they wouldn't mind just mentioning that the photographs will be taken straight after the ceremony and that they should follow the photographer out of the room.

Guess what....200 people who have been controlled for 30 minutes by the Registrar, are still going to be controlled by them and the majority will follow you. As always, there are exceptions to this rule, in this case make sure that you have the Bride and Groom in tow. Everyone will follow them anyway.

So, you have photographed the Bride and Groom leaving the room and you need a shot of them on their own just outside the door to the venue. Prepare your assistant in advance and have them stand behind the newly married couple. The assistants' job here is to stop the crowd for a second while you get this shot. Do it quickly, and then let everyone out.

Once they are all outside, be on the lookout for confetti. Ask people if they have any and if they do, make sure that you are in control of when and where it is used.

Ideally you will have identified an area close by where the confetti can be thrown. You now need to speak to the Bride and Groom and let them know what is happening. Then have all of the people with confetti form two lines. You want the Bride and Groom to walk down the middle. Once you are set up and ready you need all of the confetti to be thrown on a count of three.

Have your camera set on continuous focus, continuous shots and a reasonably high speed shutter (light permitting) and on the count of three, take as many shots as you can in the time you have, keeping the couple in the viewfinder all of the time.

You should end up with a few good useable shots and also some that can be cropped later on to get close ups.

Alternative venues – The Church wedding

So far, I have taken you step by step through a wedding that has been set in one place; everything and everyone that you need to photograph have been in one location. Church weddings are slightly different. The first obstacle is proximity. Your Bride and Groom will be arriving from different locations and by different means. Your reception is going to be in a second location, and if the Bride requires preparation shots, she will be in a third location. In this instance an assistant is a necessity, even if their only job is to drive you from one location to the other.

We will assume for now that you have an assistant and that you have a church wedding at 12 noon.

Your assistant will need to be with the bride at her home no later than 10:30. This will give him / her about 1 hour to complete the photographs before the Bride leaves for the church.

Whilst this is happening you will need to be at the church and getting yourself ready. You will need to look over the whole area, decide where your photographs are going to be taken bearing in mind that they will be taken 2 hours from now and that the sun will have moved during that time. When you are making this decision be aware of things that only usually appear in Church yards, like grave stones, as these can really spoil the mood of a wedding photograph. Also lookout for signs, churches have a habit of posting huge signs with messages that are not always conducive to the mood of a wedding.

You need to speak to the Vicar / Priest as soon as it is possible. Just as before with the Registrar, he or she will have their own rules on what can be photographed and what cannot. They will all be pretty much unanimous in the fact that you cannot use flash. So once you have the rules, get into the church and take some test shots. Find the best setting for your camera using only the available light.

Now you need to be outside waiting for the arrival of the Groom, usually he will arrive before the guests. So for a 12 noon wedding, I would expect the Groom to arrive around 11:15 along with his Groomsmen. As before, check they are dressed appropriately and get their photographs done and out of the way. Whilst on this subject, please make sure that you have asked about the Grooms method of arrival. In most cases he will just get a lift from the best man, but occasionally he will want to be delivered in something a little more exotic, like a Ferrari. If this is the case, please make sure that you are in the right place at the right time to photograph his arrival.

Once all of the Grooms images are done with, focus on the guests who by now will be arriving. Just as before, try to get them in groups / couples as they arrive.

1130hrs – Your Bride will be thinking about leaving for the church, most guests will have arrived at the church and your Groom will be at the front of the church about to endure the longest 30 minutes of his life. A thousand things are going through his mind. Will she turn up? Will I say the right things? Have I got the right day? Have I got the right church? Do I look fat in this suit? Did I set the machine to record that movie? And at least 995 more things besides. All of these thoughts will create expressions ranging from abject fear and uncontrollable sadness to euphoria. Try and capture them all.

11:45 – Your Bride is about to arrive. All guests should be inside the church, you need to be outside the church awaiting her arrival. It is also worth mentioning at this point that your assistant, assuming that you have had the presence of mind to get one, will arrive AFTER the bride because he or she will have been taking photographs of the Bride leaving. He or she will also need time to find a parking space because all of the spaces will have been occupied by the guests. This means that unlike the Civil ceremony described earlier you will most likely be on your own at this point. It will be your job to photograph the Brides arrival, the car, carriage, motorcycle that she arrived in or on and the Brides father or equivalent. The Bridesmaids should also be present at this time so make sure that they are included in the photographs.

The vicar or Priest will come and greet the Bride. While he is doing this get into the church and in position to photograph the entourage as they enter the building and the walk down the aisle. Just as with the civil ceremony, you need to get as much detail as possible culminating in a line at the front of the alter of Bride, Groom, Best man and Brides father.

Now get out of the way and follow the instructions given to you by the Vicar or Priest. Usually as a minimum they will allow you to photograph the exchange of rings and also the kiss at the end of the ceremony.

During the ceremony try to keep out of sight, use the long lens to get as much as you are allowed, don't forget the congregation. Hymns are good for masking the sound of the shutter - not so good if you have a radio link with your assistant who can't resist the urge to join in during the choir's rendition of Jerusalem!

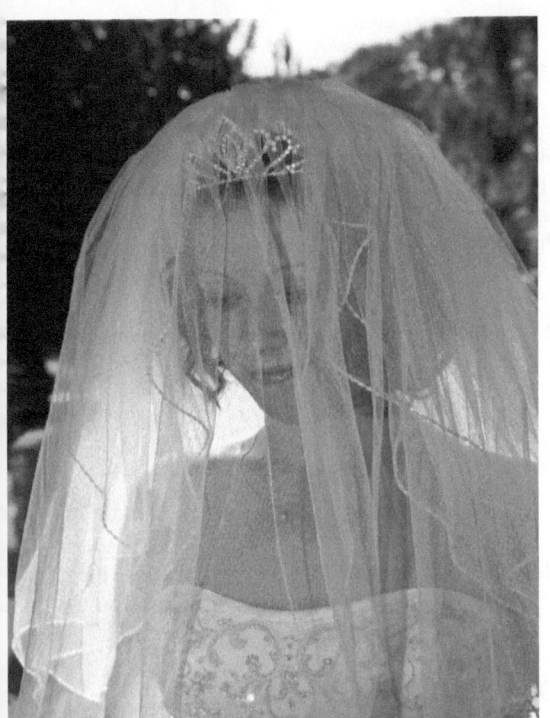

The group Shots

You now need to direct the couple to the area where you intend to take your group photographs. This takes a little time as you need to gradually get them to follow you, but they are being congratulated by the guests. Concentrate on the Bride, it is her list and she will want it to be completed, gradually lead her to where she needs to be and the rest will follow.

As you are doing this, notice what the other guests are doing. A select few will be trying to get away to the bar; others will be hiding behind anything big enough to hide them because they don't want to be in the photographs. Odds are that all of these people will be on the list; your job is to round them up and ask them to join the group.

Some Brides will ask for a shot of the whole group, some won't. Either way you will need to take this shot for two reasons.
1. She will want the photograph later anyway.
2. It is the only way that you can guarantee having every single guest in your sight.

Now that you have them all in front of you, take the group shot and then quickly grab your second camera with the long lens and work along the line taking close-ups of as many people as you can.

Next, begin splitting the group into the smaller groups from the brides list. If your assistant does this for you, you can stay at the front of the crowd and retain a certain amount of control. If you approach the crowd they will disperse and again you will lose them, if you stay in position they will usually stay in front of you.

Depending on the list you should be able to this as quickly and painlessly as possible, and please don't shout at them.

For instance, by default the couples family will have gravitated to the centre of the group to be near the Bride and Groom. This is because they feel that they are more important than the couples friends. Also, close family will be nearer to the couple than distant family for the same reason. Use this psychology to your advantage.

Ask all family to stay where they are and all friends to move to one side and line up for a photograph. Now photograph the Bride, Groom and family. Now ask everyone to stay where they are and ask the Bride and Groom to move to the other group, now take the same shot but with friends. Again ask everyone to stay where they are.

Next, split the family group into his and hers, and ask the couple to move once again and stand in turn with both groups, do the same with the friends.

You have now taken six large group photographs in under five minutes and you only had to move two people.

You now have four groups of people and the Bride and Groom. Keep the Bride and Groom with you and ask your assistant to illicit the help of the Groomsmen and Bridesmaids to gather the remaining people on the list. Most of the bridal party will have either forgotten or lost their copy of the list, this is why you made copies the night before the wedding. Hand them out and ask them to find the people you need.

They should be able to do this quickly as between them they will know everyone by name and they will have four distinct groups to choose from i.e.

- Brides family
- Grooms family
- Brides friends
- Grooms friends

This entire process needs to be complete in less than 30 minutes, after this you will lose the crowd forever. Any shots not taken during this time may need to be taken later on unless you have an extremely patient group of people.

Once the groups are complete, you will need to photograph the Bridal party and then the Bride and Groom. Everyone else can go.

If there is time, give your Bride and Groom a break. Let them know what is happening next and let the bridal party know too. Give them and you 10 or 15 minutes if you can afford it and then they will far more relaxed for the next step.

The Bridal party

So far, every time you have set up a photograph there will have been at least one budding photographer copying your shot, and 30 people with a smartphone doing the same. Some of the photographs that you have set up will be on social media before you began taking the groups shots. Accept it, live with it; it was always going to happen.

Now is your opportunity to create some images that no one else will have seen, no one else can copy, and no one except you can post on social media. Because you have sent all of the budding photographers and all of the smart phones to the bar.

Use this time well.

Once the break is over, gather your Bridal party together and take them to a different area within the grounds.

For the Bridal party, use a similar technique as you did for the group shots. Start with the whole group, break it down into;

- Bride, Groom and Groomsmen
- Groom with Groomsmen
- Bride with Groomsmen
- Bride and Groom with bridesmaids
- Bride with Bridesmaids
- Groom with Bridesmaids

Whilst these people are lined up, take the group and then ask them to take two steps away from each other, creating a gap.

Now take three shots of each person

- Full length
- Three quarter
- Close up / portrait

And now thank them and let them go.

The Bride and Groom

Check the time. Ideally you could do with about half an hour minimum so that you can spend some time taking some memorable photographs of the Bride and Groom without the guests present.

Hopefully you will have found a nice area in the grounds to use for this. Ideally with a few stunning backgrounds, some kind of seating, lakes and rivers are always good and if you can get all this and still include the venue building in the photographs then you're doing well.

To help you with this part it is a good idea to have a few sheets of photographs that you either like from another photographer or a few that you have taken yourself, or a mix. Have them printed off in contact sheets so that you can show the Bride and Groom what you are trying to achieve, it makes it a lot easier for them to pose if they have a picture to look at first.

Again your assistant is invaluable here. He or she will become your art director. The assistant can pose the couple using the contact sheets, paying attention to the Brides dress, flowers and hair and you can position yourself for the perfect shot.

Do not forget to get some nice full length shots of each of them and also some nice portraits.

If you are intending to produce an album as part of your offer, bear in mind that a lot of these Bride and Groom shots will take pride of place in the middle of the album. Make them perfect, as large a file as possible and this is the only time during any wedding photography that I would advocate checking the image on the camera screen before moving on to the next pose.

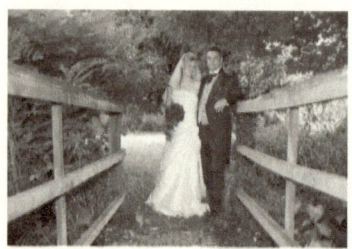 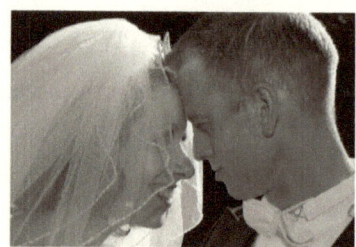

As soon as this part of the shoot is completed change the memory card. You need these to be as safe as they can be. Of all the photographs that you have taken today so far, these are your most valuable. No one else will have seen them, no one else could have copied them, and no one could have placed then on social media. Therefore, of all the images that you have taken today, these are the ones that you can sell over and over again to guests, friends of guests and of course the Bride and Groom as wall art.

Once done, escort the Bride and Groom back to their reception and find the organiser. Check the timings again, double check the speech times. I have lost count of how many times I have been told that the speeches will be at the end of the meal and they decide at the last minute to do them at the beginning.

Go back to the room where the meal is to be served and check they haven't added anything, if they have, take photographs of it. This may be the only opportunity to get some images of the cake too while it doesn't have people standing around it.

Candid photographs

During the time before the meal the guests will be mingling with each other and with the Bride and Groom. Use this time to take some candid photographs. Use the long lens, the further away you are, the more natural the shots will be.

Also be on the lookout for anything unusual, or amusing. Children will usually do both, and people will pay for photographs of their children. Lookout for impromptu groups too. Family's will create their own group photographs, get in there and take the shot, once they see you doing this others will ask you to take photographs of their family too, they may pay for these later on.

While all this is going on, remember to keep an eye on where the Bride is, it is still her day, so include her in the candid photographs and family groups.

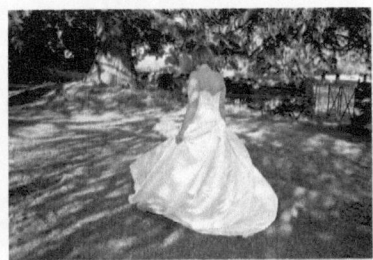 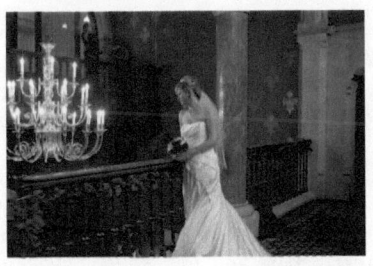

Time for the Wedding breakfast

If the wedding is being organised correctly, the organiser should be running to time and aware that it is now time to seat everyone. This may involve a receiving line, if it does you need to get a position opposite to the Bride and Groom and get shots as the guests file past. These images are generally quite boring and rarely make it to the album, but occasionally something funny or memorable happens and it's then worth doing.

We are assuming that the speeches are going to be given at the end of the meal.

As soon as the receiving line is finished, the guests will hopefully be seated. The Bride and Groom will make their entrance very shortly. The organiser should announce them in and ask everyone to stand. Position yourself so that you can see the doorway that they are going to walk from and also the table at which they are going sit. Photograph them as they enter the room, as they move to their seat and again once they are seated.

Now you need to get around the room and take the table shots. Try and make sure that there are no empty seats and position yourself so that you can get everyone on the table into the shot. It is a good idea to get this position and then ask your assistant to get the guests attention by asking them to look at you.

Once all of the tables have been photographed you can have a rest. Check with the organiser so that you know exactly how much time you have and make sure that you both know exactly that time the speeches will be, also let the Bride and Groom know that you are going to get some food and that you will be back in time for the speeches. Usually you will have about an hour or more before the speeches, plenty of time to go and get something to eat.

Your assistant has worked hard today so make sure that you buy them a nice meal.

When you come back to the venue, go straight to the room and check with staff on the progress of the meal. You may need to wait outside of the room until they are ready for the speeches. As soon as you think that they are about to begin you need to get into a position where you can see the top table, but also make sure that you're not in everyone's way, remember the guests will want to see and take photographs too. Also, bear in mind that the guests will do a lot of standing up and toasting the Bride and Groom, so make sure that when they do, you are not going to behind them all and unable to get a photograph.

The Speeches

These can take anywhere up an hour, but hopefully they will be short and sweet. All you can do here is try to get reactions to things that are being said. It can be easier if you have an assistant because one of you can concentrate on the Bride, Groom and the person speaking whilst the other one points towards the guests. This way you shouldn't miss anything.

Listen to what is being said. You should be able to anticipate punch lines and tears. Make sure that you know who the immediate family are, and where they are. Use the long lens for most of these shots as the images should about expressions and reactions. If the speaker is talking about someone in particular, find that person and frame them in your viewfinder. Hold still and wait for the reaction, it's your job as the photographer to capture moments that the bride, groom & their family are missing. Who's laughing, who's crying? What did the bride look like as her father was speaking?

Throughout the speeches keep an eye out for flowers and gifts being given to various people, these make nice, and sometimes funny photographs.

Once the speeches are done your next milestone will be the cutting of the cake. This tends to happen very suddenly so be sure to check with the organiser to agree a time when it will be done. In a lot of cases it tends to happen just before the first dance as they will use the dance floor to get the cake into the middle of the room. Speak to the DJ if there is one because odds are that he or she will be the one to announce it. Once you are sure how long you have before the cake cutting you are again free to go off and get some candid shots.

People by this time will have drunk a little more and instead of running away from the camera they will be hounding you to take their photographs. Many people will be trying to get their own little groups as earlier, get the photo too, but don't be too precious about the photography, offer to use their own equipment here and there to take their photographs, people will like that they have a professional photograph on their phone, and later on in the evening they will remember what you did and be more helpful when you need them to pose once again. They are also more likely to remember you the next time someone asks them for a recommendation.

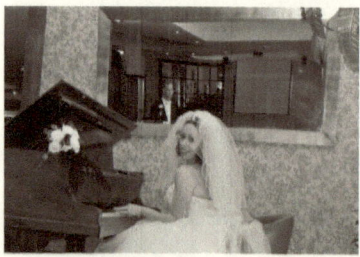 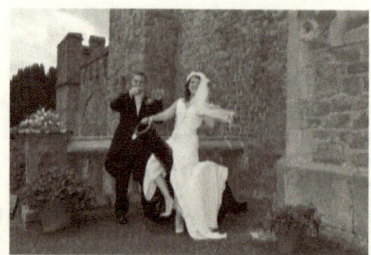

The Cake

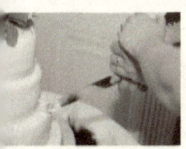

Once the time has come for the cake cutting first job is to make sure that they have a knife, I have lost count of the amount of venues that forget to provide one. Also, you will need to ask the Bride and Groom if they intend to actually cut the cake or if they are just going to pretend. The reason for this question is that if they intend to actually cut the cake, you could use a few shots before they actually do cut it.

Position yourself so that you are directly in front of the couple and can see both them and the cake, the guests will move around you and hopefully won't stand in front of you. Have the Bride and Groom hold the knife over the cake as if they are about to cut it and looking at you, looking at each other, looking at the cake. Then ask them to just cut the cake and do what they want. You should now have some nicely posed shots and some natural shots too. As with the speeches, it's always a good idea to have your assistant taking photographs in the opposite direction so that you also have pictures of the guests and their reactions.

Once the cake is done with, make sure that it is removed from the dance floor or to a safe place by the venue staff. I have seen them forget to do this too!

The first dance

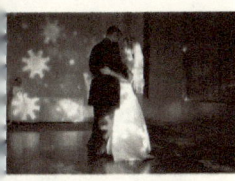

This can be tricky, what you are aiming for here are some nice long shots and some nice close ups. Odds are that the room will be dark, very dark. What you don't want is a series of full flash shots that light up the entire room and bleach out the Bride and Groom. You also don't want the shots to be so dark that you can't see anyone. If you shoot without flash even at a high ISO you will either get too much movement blur, or too much photograph noise.

However, all is not lost. Your camera manufacturer has spent several millions of pounds or dollars perfecting the camera that you now hold in your hand. Its software is more than capable of dealing with this issue for you and all it needs from you is a little help. Turn your flash head to bounce of a wall or ceiling taking care not to point it directly at someone's face, Set your camera on 'P' for programmed (not 'P' for professional as many would have you believe).

Now line up and take your shots. If they look a little dark turn the flash a little, if they are too bright turn the flash away. The camera will do the rest. Even if the images don't look perfect in the camera, a little post processing will bring them back exactly how you need them to be.

As the couple 'glide' around the dancefloor try to get expressions, the Grooms hand on her waist, capture the atmosphere of the dance. Some of these shots will look good in black and white too so think about this when taking them.

Usually about half way through the first dance some of the guests will join in, time to step back and take any photographs you can of the people on the dancefloor.

Night time guests

As the night time guests begin to arrive keep an eye out for new faces, if you can try and get them in the groups in which they have arrived. Remember that these people won't have had a drink yet and will be reluctant to have photographs taken. This will all change in about an hour. As the new guests settle in they will begin to congregate in groups this is a good time to go around the room or venue again and ask people to pose for photographs, usually by this time they will be quite accommodating.

Don't forget the smokers! You will usually find groups of people outside the venue (weather permitting) so be sure to have a look around and include them in the photographs where possible.

Low light shots

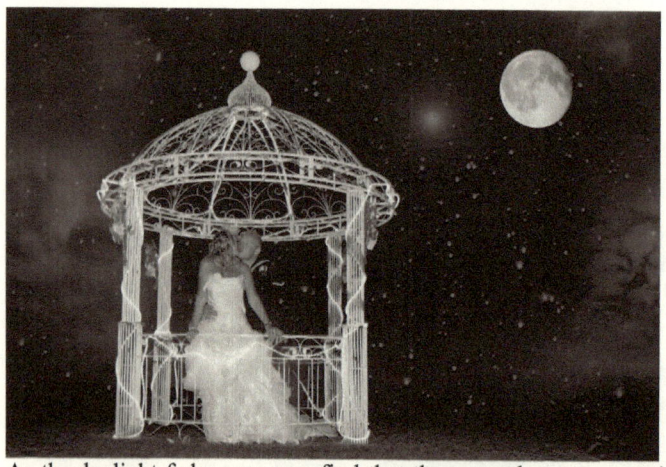

As the daylight fades you may find that the venue has areas outside that have been lit nicely with fairy lights or gas burners, there may be a lake or pond that has been illuminated, or a gazebo. If there is anything like this these will make very nice additions to the collection. If you locate the Bride and Groom and ask nicely I'm sure that they won't mind giving you another 20 minutes of their time in order to get a few nice atmospheric shots. Use a similar technique to the one employed during the first dance shots. You could even try a few test shots before asking the couple to come with you so that when you do the photographs for real you are quicker and they are not delayed so long.

Also look out for anywhere indoors where you might be able to get a similar effect. Large mirrors are good as long you or your flash are not in the reflection, and the reflection of the venue's interior is not too fussy or too plain.

Time to leave them to it

By now most people will probably be pleased to see you leave, they can relax, have a drink and enjoy the evening secure in the knowledge that you are not going to be photographing them from the other side of the room.

Find your Bride and Groom, tell them that you have everything you need and ask them if there is anything else that they need before you leave, if there is get it done, if not say your goodbyes, thank them for a lovely day and let them know that their images will be ready as soon as they are back from honeymoon.

Secure the images

When you return to your car, do not just put the camera in the boot and drive off. Make sure that all memory cards are stored in a secure container and not left in the cameras. Make sure that the card container is safe and then secure the rest of your equipment.

Home at last

It has been a long day, you are tired, hungry and thirsty, but the day isn't over yet. All of the equipment needs to be secured and not left in the car. Imagine the car being stolen along with your livelihood and all of the days images – you now need to back up every single image before your day is complete.

I will always COPY all of the images from the cards onto the computer as soon as I am home and leave the originals on the cards, this gives me two copies. Then I will back up the computer onto an external drive giving me three copies and finally I will back up the external drive onto a second drive leaving me with four complete copies. The second external drive will then be stored offsite as soon as possible as an archive backup just in case anything happens to the other copies.

Once you know that your images are safe, you can relax a little.

Post processing

How you produce the final article is up to you and whatever you have agreed with the Bride and Groom. Some people will simply produce the images onto a DVD, some put them onto a memory stick and some people will print every image and give them to the Bride and Groom as proofs some of which will be placed into an album later on. The choice of albums is endless, from digital albums right through to an album where each image is stuck onto a page. Yours and their choice will usually come down to cost.

Whichever way you are going to present your images will dictate how you process them.

Software

There are various software packages and you should choose the one that suits you best. I have found that <u>Adobe® Lightroom</u> is the best for me with <u>Adobe Photoshop®</u> for any special effects that I may wish to add later.

When you are processing the images delete any duplicates, you don't want to bombard the Bride and Groom with hundreds of images that look the same. Do not be afraid to delete any image that you are not happy with, if you're not happy, they won't be either. <u>Adobe® Lightroom</u> is very good for this as it edits a virtual image and not the original, it also deletes virtually and not from your drive, so if you change your mind you will always have the original image if needed.

Once you have processed all of the images and you are happy with the results, back them up and leave them for a couple of days. Then go back and look again, if you are still pleased it is worth having someone else take a look in case you missed anything.

Things to check

Make sure that every single image that you are going to present to the Bride and Groom:

- ❖ Is sharp and the colours are true
- ❖ Does not contain any red-eye
- ❖ Is not a duplicate
- ❖ Is in the correct chronological order

Further photographs to aim for:

The wedding breakfast room

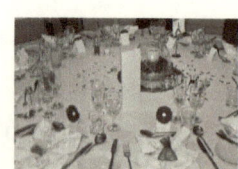

- ❖ Chair decoration
- ❖ Table decoration
- ❖ Wedding favours
- ❖ Anything that has been printed with the bride and grooms name
- ❖ Balloons
- ❖ Gifts either on the tables or stored for handing out later
- ❖ Seating plan
- ❖ The cake, if present
- ❖ The whole room

Some or all of these images will also make nice backgrounds for a digital album.

Signing the register

❖ Place the Brides bouquet nicely at the front of the table
❖ Bride and Groom with the register looking at each other
❖ Bride and Groom as above but kissing
❖ Bride holding the pen as if to sign with the groom looking at her
❖ Groom holding the pen with the bride looking at him
❖ Bride and groom with witnesses.
❖ Bride and groom with bridal party
❖ Close up of bride and groom holding the pen

Once you have your shots, allow the guests to move in and take their own. Position yourself so that you can still take photographs with the long lens as they will relax more with their guests and you will get some nice images.

The Bride and Groom

❖ Sitting – If there is a bench or similar have them sitting close to each other, looking at each other, kissing, ask them to talk to each other and take images of the conversation – this gives natural images and expressions.
❖ Standing – Use your location to its best advantage; lakes, the venue, rivers and any nice scenery will make good back-drops. Look out for undesirable objects in your sightline and move around as needed to avoid them in your shots.
❖ Moving – Have the bride and groom walk away from you holding hands and photograph them from the back, ask them to stop and look back at you, then do the same from the front as they approach you.
❖ Spinning – If she is able, ask the bride to spin quickly so that her dress swirls, if she has a veil allow this to move also (photograph this at high speed and choose the best one or two images)
❖ The veil – If there is slight breeze, ask your assistant to lift the veil out and away from the bride, pose the bride so that she is sideways on to the camera, when you are ready ask your assistant to let go of the veil and get out of the way quickly, this creates and image of the veil and gives movement to the image.
❖ Gazebo – If there is one, use it. It will frame the bride and groom nicely. A small bridge will do the same – use whatever you have at the venue to enhance your images otherwise you may end up with a photograph of two people standing in a field.

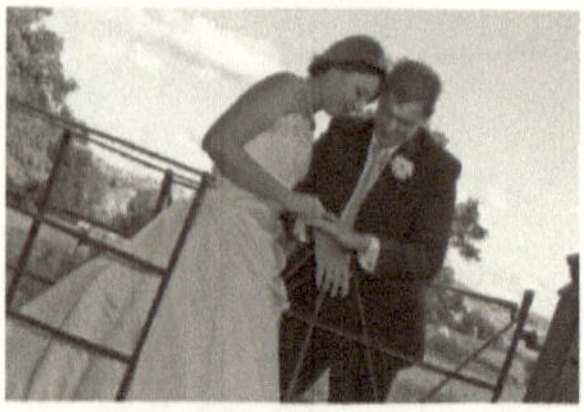

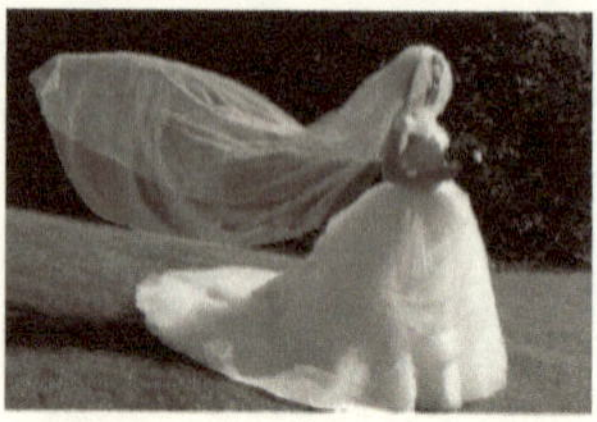

Hopefully you now have all the equipment, and all of the information that you need to successfully photograph a wedding. Your key to success will start with meticulous planning, testing and checking equipment and your ability to keep calm under pressure.

Throughout this guide I have constantly mentioned the role and importance of an assistant. I cannot stress strongly enough the importance of having a good assistant. They can make the difference between an 'ok' wedding shoot, and an exceptional one, and are worth every penny that you spend on them.

Good luck with your wedding photography, and please note that I am available for 1 to 1 training and can be contacted at the email address below. My assistant, however, is not for hire.

gnhphotography@btinternet.com